FIERCE FIGHTERS
PREDATORS

FIERCE FIGHTERS
PREDATORS

NATURE'S TOUGHEST GO HEAD TO HEAD

BY PAUL BECK AND LEE MARTIN

becker&mayer! kids

CONTENT

FIERCE FIGHTERS

Some hunt on land and some in the water. Some are huge, and some are tiny. Some chase their prey, and some wait in ambush to surprise it. But all the animals you'll meet in this book have one thing in common: they're fierce fighters that use their own special weapons to hunt and defend themselves. Many of these predators will never meet in the wild, but here, you'll get to see what would happen if they battled each other in head-to-head contests.

GRAY WOLF

PREDATORS

Predators are animals that hunt and eat other animals. Some, like sperm whales and praying mantises, eat only animals that they catch. Others, like grizzly bears and gray wolves, are *omnivores* that also eat plants. Still others, like bald eagles and great white sharks, are also scavengers as well as hunters, both catching live prey and eating animals that are already dead.

LIFE AT THE TOP

Animals like grizzly bears, lions, sharks, and orcas are *apex predators*. "Apex" means "top," and these hunters are the top predators in their habitats. They're always the hunter and never the prey. Other predators become prey themselves—puff adders get eaten by honey badgers, and seals get eaten by orcas. And some, like young Komodo dragons, can even become prey for larger members of their own kind.

APEX PREDATORS

GRIZZLY BEAR

LION

SHARK

ORCA

GRIZZLY BEAR VS. MOUNTAIN LION

GRIZZLY BEAR

One of the largest mammals in North America, a grizzly can stand as tall as 7 feet (2.1 m). Grizzlies have claws as long as human fingers, which they use when fighting, and they can reach speeds of 35 mph (56 kph).

SCIENTIFIC NAME	*Ursus arctos horribilis*
LENGTH (WITHOUT TAIL)	5–8 feet (1.5–2.4 m)
TYPICAL PREY	Salmon, moose
PREDATOR STYLE	Opportunistic; feeds on almost any animal that comes its way
HABITAT	Northern North America

GRIZZLY BEAR

STATS		
SPEED		7
STRENGTH		9
BRAINS	5	
ATTACK		7
DEFENSE		8

THE SHOWDOWN

Two top predators—one brawny and the other sleek—go head to head. The mountain lion stalks and ambushes, and the grizzly relies on its powerful forearms and formidable claws to grab and slash.

MOUNTAIN LION

Strong and stealthy, the mountain lion has legs designed for quick acceleration and pouncing, and sharp teeth for tearing prey. The mountain lion stalks and leaps, clutching the prey with its paws and biting the back of its neck.

MOUNTAIN LION

STATS

8	SPEED	
6	STRENGTH	
8	BRAINS	
8	ATTACK	
7	DEFENSE	

SCIENTIFIC NAME	*Puma concolor*
LENGTH (WITHOUT TAIL)	3.25–5.25 feet (1–1.6 m)
TYPICAL PREY	Deer, coyotes, porcupines, raccoons
PREDATOR STYLE	Stalks, pounces; hides kill and returns to eat for several days
HABITAT	Canada, much of the United States, and Central and South America

WHO WINS?
SEE PAGE 110.

ORCA VS. GREAT WHITE SHARK

ORCA

Orcas, or killer whales, live and hunt together in groups called pods. They live in more parts of the world than any other marine mammal.

SCIENTIFIC NAME	*Orcinus orca*
LENGTH	20–32 feet (6.1–9.8 m)
TYPICAL PREY	Fish, seals, sea lions, porpoises, smaller whales
PREDATOR STYLE	Pack hunter; uses echolocation (sonar) to find and pursue prey
WATER TYPE	Salt

ORCA

STATS		
SPEED		9
STRENGTH		10
BRAINS		9
ATTACK		10
DEFENSE		10

THE SPLASHDOWN

It's an epic battle between the ocean's apex predators! Orcas are the biggest members of the dolphin family, with males weighing as much as 11 tons (9,979 kg). The great white shark is the world's biggest predatory fish.

GREAT WHITE SHARK

This shark usually swims just under the surface, then attacks with a rush from below. One razor-toothed bite can cut through flesh, bone, and even turtle shells.

GREAT WHITE SHARK

STATS

7	SPEED	
10	STRENGTH	
5	BRAINS	
10	ATTACK	
10	DEFENSE	

SCIENTIFIC NAME	*Carcharodon carcharias*
LENGTH	14–20 feet (4.3–6.1 m)
TYPICAL PREY	Seals, sea lions, dolphins, large fish
PREDATOR STYLE	Attacks with a surprise rush from below
WATER TYPE	Salt

WHO WINS? SEE PAGE 110.

AMERICAN ALLIGATOR VS. SALTWATER CROCODILE

AMERICAN ALLIGATOR

This hunter has a champion chomp. A big alligator's jaws clamp down with 2,000 pounds (907 kg) of force, more than 16 times the biting power of a human.

SCIENTIFIC NAME	*Alligator mississippiensis*
LENGTH	8–15 feet (2.4–4.6 m)
TYPICAL PREY	Fish, turtles, snakes, small mammals, carrion
PREDATOR STYLE	Ambush hunter
WATER TYPE	Fresh

AMERICAN ALLIGATOR

STATS		
SPEED	6	
STRENGTH		10
BRAINS	4	
ATTACK		9
DEFENSE		9

THE SPLASHDOWN

It's the ultimate crocodilian splashdown, with the toughest reptile of North America going up against the biggest croc of them all, from half a world away. Can the American hunter hold its own against the largest reptile in the world?

SALTWATER CROCODILE

Like other crocodilians, the "saltie" hunts by ambush, often lying in wait near the shore, then lunging out to drag large animals into the water.

SALTWATER CROCODILE

STATS

6	SPEED	
10	STRENGTH	
4	BRAINS	
10	ATTACK	
10	DEFENSE	

SCIENTIFIC NAME	*Crocodylus porosus*
LENGTH	10–20 feet (3–6.1 m)
TYPICAL PREY	Anything it can catch, including fish, reptiles, and large mammals
PREDATOR STYLE	Ambush hunter
WATER TYPE	Salt/Fresh

WHO WINS? SEE PAGE 110.

FAT-TAILED SCORPION

The scorpion has a scary set of claws and a curved tail with a venomous stinger. The smaller the scorpion, the stronger its venom—some scorpions' venom is strong enough to kill a human.

SCIENTIFIC NAME	*Androctonus australis*
LENGTH	1.5–4 inches (4–10 cm)
TYPICAL PREY	Insects, mice, frogs
PREDATOR STYLE	Grabs prey; injects venom
HABITAT	Northern Africa and the Middle East

FAT-TAILED SCORPION

STAT		
SPEED		8
STRENGTH		7
BRAINS	2	
ATTACK		8
DEFENSE		8

THE SHOWDOWN

Scorpions have lived on Earth for more than 400 million years. Some species of tarantula feast on animals as large as birds and mice. What happens when the armored survivor meets the fearless fighter?

HORNED BABOON TARANTULA

For spiders, tarantulas are enormous. They don't build webs but instead set traps to capture their prey, or they hunt at night by sneaking up and attacking.

HORNED BABOON TARANTULA

STATS	
8	SPEED
7	STRENGTH
2	BRAINS
7	ATTACK
5	DEFENSE

SCIENTIFIC NAME	*Ceratogyrus brachycephalus*
LENGTH	2.5–3 inches (6–7.6 cm)
TYPICAL PREY	Insects, mice, small lizards
PREDATOR STYLE	Ambushes; crushes prey or injects with venom
HABITAT	Southern Africa

WHO WINS? SEE PAGE 110.

NILE CROCODILE VS. HIPPOPOTAMUS

NILE CROCODILE

Nile crocodiles will hunt anything they can catch, including large mammals like zebras, wildebeests, and even humans. They can eat half their own weight in a single meal.

SCIENTIFIC NAME	*Crocodylus niloticus*
LENGTH	7–16 feet (2.1–4.9 m)
TYPICAL PREY	Mostly fish, also mammals, birds, and other crocodiles
PREDATOR STYLE	Ambush hunter; sometimes hunts in groups
WATER TYPE	Fresh

NILE CROCODILE

STATS		
SPEED		6
STRENGTH		10
BRAINS	4	
ATTACK		10
DEFENSE		10

THE SPLASHDOWN

Frequent foes face off in an African river battle. The Nile crocodile is the second-largest croc in the world. Its prey includes small hippos. The hippo may be a vegetarian, but it can defend itself in a fight with its enormous size and dagger-sharp canine teeth.

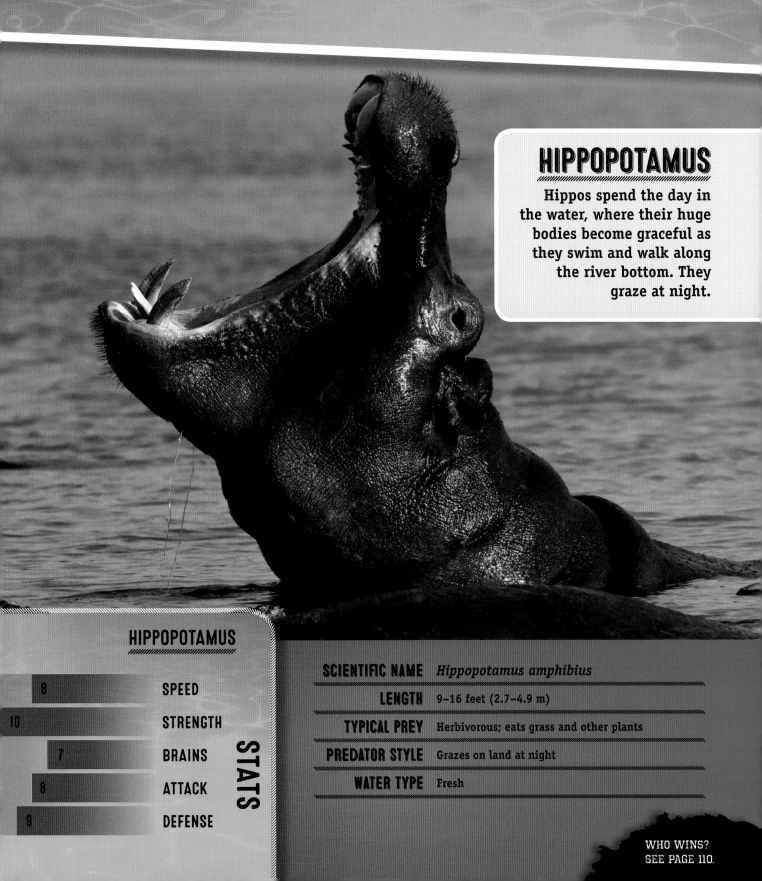

HIPPOPOTAMUS

Hippos spend the day in the water, where their huge bodies become graceful as they swim and walk along the river bottom. They graze at night.

HIPPOPOTAMUS

STATS

8	SPEED
10	STRENGTH
7	BRAINS
8	ATTACK
9	DEFENSE

SCIENTIFIC NAME	*Hippopotamus amphibius*
LENGTH	9–16 feet (2.7–4.9 m)
TYPICAL PREY	Herbivorous; eats grass and other plants
PREDATOR STYLE	Grazes on land at night
WATER TYPE	Fresh

WHO WINS?
SEE PAGE 110.

HONEY BADGER VS. WOLVERINE

HONEY BADGER

This fierce creature will attack any animal and has been known to steal a lion's kill. The honey badger is equipped with long claws, sharp teeth, and loose-fitting skin that allows it to twist away from attackers.

SCIENTIFIC NAME	*Mellivora capensis*
LENGTH (WITHOUT TAIL)	3 feet (91 cm)
TYPICAL PREY	Rodents, termites, snakes, and other reptiles
PREDATOR STYLE	Tracks and attacks
HABITAT	Greater part of sub-Saharan Africa through the Middle East, to southern Russia, and east to India and Nepal

HONEY BADGER

STATS

SPEED	7
STRENGTH	6
BRAINS	6
ATTACK	7
DEFENSE	6

THE SHOWDOWN

Neither of these two feisty animals from the weasel family will back down in a fight. In fact, the *Guinness Book of World Records* named the honey badger the most fearless animal on Earth. And the wolverine is known for harassing bears, mountain lions, and wolves!

WOLVERINE

The wolverine is a fearsome predator that will eat almost anything. The wolverine's padded paws and long claws allow it to dig for prey, as well as fight off challengers. Its teeth and jaws are designed for crushing bone and frozen carrion.

WOLVERINE

STATS

5	SPEED
8	STRENGTH
6	BRAINS
7	ATTACK
8	DEFENSE

SCIENTIFIC NAME	*Gulo gulo*
LENGTH (WITHOUT TAIL)	2–3 feet (61–91 cm)
TYPICAL PREY	Rodents, rabbits, carrion
PREDATOR STYLE	Ambushes and pounces
HABITAT	Northern North America and northern Europe through Asia

WHO WINS? SEE PAGE 110.

POLAR BEAR VS. WALRUS

POLAR BEAR

The polar bear is the largest land predator, but it does all of its hunting in or around the ocean. Its scientific name means "sea bear."

SCIENTIFIC NAME	*Ursus maritimus*
LENGTH	6.5–8.5 feet (2–2.6 m)
TYPICAL PREY	Seals, walruses, small whales, birds, carrion, plants
PREDATOR STYLE	Waits at ice edge to ambush surfacing seals; stalks hauled-out seals from the ice or swims up from underwater for a surprise attack
WATER TYPE	Salt

POLAR BEAR

STATS		
SPEED	7	
STRENGTH		10
BRAINS	8	
ATTACK		10
DEFENSE		10

THE SPLASHDOWN

Two old enemies meet in an arctic splashdown! Polar bears will prey on young walruses, but a full-grown adult is another matter. These huge relatives of seals and sea lions come equipped with long tusks and can weigh more than 1 ton (907 kg).

WALRUS

Both male and female walruses have tusks. Males will use their tusks as weapons to defend territory and to protect harems of females during mating season.

WALRUS

STATS

8	SPEED
8	STRENGTH
8	BRAINS
6	ATTACK
7	DEFENSE

SCIENTIFIC NAME	*Odobenus rosmarus*
LENGTH	7–11 feet (2.1–3.4 m)
TYPICAL PREY	Clams, mussels, crabs, worms, snails, and other ocean-floor invertebrates
PREDATOR STYLE	Dives to the ocean floor, feels with its whiskers along the bottom to locate prey in murky water
WATER TYPE	Salt

WHO WINS?
SEE PAGE 110.

HUNTER HABITATS

A habitat is a home. It's the environment where an animal lives. There are five main types: aquatic (water) habitats, tundra (the arctic and high mountains), deserts, forests, and grasslands. Predators live in every type.

DESERT PREDATORS

Deserts are the driest habitats. The most well-known deserts are hot, dry places like the Sahara in Africa. But desert habitats also include semiarid (partly dry) places like the sagebrush country of the western United States. Some predators, like the flat-tailed scorpion, live only in the desert. Others, like the bobcat and red fox, can be found there as well as in other habitats.

Here are some of the special weapons used by desert hunters:

VENOMOUS STING

FAT-TAILED SCORPION

SHARP TEETH

DINGO

CRUSHING JAWS

HONEY BADGER

ACROBATIC POUNCE

RED FOX

PAWS & CLAWS

BOBCAT

VENOMOUS BITE

BLACK WIDOW SPIDER

BLUE-RINGED OCTOPUS VS. REEF STONEFISH

BLUE-RINGED OCTOPUS

This pint-size predator displays its bright blue rings when threatened or alarmed. It produces two types of venom: one for prey and one for defense.

SCIENTIFIC NAME	*Hapalochlaena maculosa*
LENGTH	Up to 8 inches (20 cm) total length, including arms. Its mantle (head) is 2.5 inches (6 cm)
TYPICAL PREY	Crabs and shrimp
PREDATOR STYLE	Bites or spits its venom into the water around prey—scientists aren't sure
WATER TYPE	Salt

BLUE-RINGED OCTOPUS

STATS		
SPEED		5
STRENGTH		4
BRAINS		7
ATTACK		7
DEFENSE		10

THE SPLASHDOWN

The world's most venomous mollusk and most venomous fish square off in a coral-reef battle. These predators may be small, but their self-defense toxins can be deadly to humans and large animals. Only the octopus uses its venom for hunting.

REEF STONEFISH

This camouflaged fish blends in perfectly with the rocks and coral where it lives. The 13 venomous spines on its back are strictly for defense.

REEF STONEFISH

STATS

3	SPEED	
3	STRENGTH	
3	BRAINS	
	2	ATTACK
10	DEFENSE	

SCIENTIFIC NAME	*Synanceia verrucosa*
LENGTH	10–15 inches (25–38 cm)
TYPICAL PREY	Small fish and crustaceans such as crabs
PREDATOR STYLE	Waits in ambush, then gulps down prey when it swims in range
WATER TYPE	Salt

WHO WINS? SEE PAGE 110.

CHINESE PRAYING MANTIS

Swiveling its head from side to side, the praying mantis surveys its surroundings from its camouflaged perch. Then, very quickly, it snags its prey with two front legs. The spiked legs hold the victim, while powerful jaws bite the prey and paralyze it.

SCIENTIFIC NAME	*Tenodera aridifolia sinensis*
LENGTH	4 inches (102 mm)
TYPICAL PREY	Insects, caterpillars, tree frogs, small lizards, mice
PREDATOR STYLE	Camouflage, lightning-quick attack
HABITAT	Originated in China, but now lives throughout the United States

CHINESE PRAYING MANTIS

STATS

SPEED	7
STRENGTH	7
BRAINS	5
ATTACK	8
DEFENSE	6

THE SHOWDOWN

Here are two savage, tiny predators. The Chinese praying mantis is known for its appetite and cannibalistic behavior. The Asian giant hornet is the world's largest wasp, with a quarter-inch (6 mm) stinger.

ASIAN GIANT HORNET

This 2-inch (51-mm) killer possesses a stinger, a flesh-eating toxin, and powerful mandibles that can tear the heads off prey. These hornets are fast fliers, and their stings are deadly to humans.

ASIAN GIANT HORNET

STATS

6	SPEED	
3	STRENGTH	
5	BRAINS	
8	ATTACK	
8	DEFENSE	

SCIENTIFIC NAME	*Vespa mandarinia*
LENGTH	2 inches (51 mm)
TYPICAL PREY	Honeybees
PREDATOR STYLE	Aggressive hunter
HABITAT	Temperate and tropical eastern Asia

WHO WINS?
SEE PAGE 110.

GREAT BARRACUDA

The torpedo-shaped predator has two separate sets of razor-sharp teeth. It rams into large prey with its jaws open and chomps the fish into pieces.

SCIENTIFIC NAME	*Sphyraena barracuda*
LENGTH	3–6 feet (91–183 cm)
TYPICAL PREY	Fish
PREDATOR STYLE	Hunts by sight and speed
WATER TYPE	Salt

GREAT BARRACUDA

STATS

SPEED	9
STRENGTH	6
BRAINS	5
ATTACK	7
DEFENSE	6

THE SPLASHDOWN

Two top predators face off in this coral-reef splashdown. The great barracuda is built for speed, with a slim body and a mouth bristling with pointy teeth. The gray reef shark is one of the most aggressive shark species.

GRAY REEF SHARK

The gray reef shark lives in coral-reef areas of the Pacific and Indian Oceans. This aggressive shark has been known to attack humans.

GRAY REEF SHARK

		STATS
8	SPEED	
8	STRENGTH	
5	BRAINS	
8	ATTACK	
8	DEFENSE	

SCIENTIFIC NAME	*Carcharhinus amblyrhynchos*
LENGTH	4–8 feet (1.2–2.4 m)
TYPICAL PREY	Fish, sometimes including other gray reef sharks; also squid, octopuses, crabs, and shrimp
PREDATOR STYLE	Prowls for prey near coral reefs, most often at night
WATER TYPE	Salt

WHO WINS?
SEE PAGE 110.

GOLDEN JACKAL VS. PUFF ADDER

GOLDEN JACKAL

The jackal is an able predator, able to maintain a trotting speed of about 10 mph (16 kph) for a long time. Its canine teeth are curved, perfect for biting and holding on to prey.

SCIENTIFIC NAME	*Canis aureus*
LENGTH (WITHOUT TAIL)	2.5–3 feet (.8–.9 m)
TYPICAL PREY	Reptiles, rodents, ground-dwelling birds, small antelope
PREDATOR STYLE	Intelligence, resourcefulness
HABITAT	Northern Africa, Europe, Asia

GOLDEN JACKAL

STATS

SPEED	8
STRENGTH	6
BRAINS	7
ATTACK	7
DEFENSE	6

THE SHOWDOWN

These animals inhabit some of the same areas, so it's likely they would come up against each other. In fact, some jackals specialize in hunting snakes. The puff adder has a great offense and a devastating defense: its long fangs and venomous bite.

PUFF ADDER

The puff adder is considered the most dangerous venomous snake in Africa. It has a bad temper—hissing and puffing when agitated. The puff adder is normally slow, but when upset, it strikes with amazing speed.

PUFF ADDER

STATS		
5	SPEED	
2	STRENGTH	
3	BRAINS	
8	ATTACK	
7	DEFENSE	

SCIENTIFIC NAME	*Bitis ariens*
LENGTH	3.3 feet (1 m)
TYPICAL PREY	Rodents and other small mammals, birds, lizards
PREDATOR STYLE	During the day, lies in wait; at dusk, hunts
HABITAT	Sub-Saharan Africa

WHO WINS?
SEE PAGE 110.

ELECTRIC EEL VS. RED-BELLIED PIRANHA

ELECTRIC EEL

The electric eel can deliver a zap of more than 600 volts. Nearly blind, it uses lower-voltage electrical signals to search for prey.

SCIENTIFIC NAME	*Electrophorus electricus*
LENGTH	6–8 feet (1.8–2.4 m)
TYPICAL PREY	Fish, amphibians, sometimes small birds and mammals
PREDATOR STYLE	Stuns prey with a powerful electric shock, then gulps it down
WATER TYPE	Fresh

ELECTRIC EEL

STATS

SPEED	3
STRENGTH	4
BRAINS	4
ATTACK	6
DEFENSE	8

THE SPLASHDOWN

The Amazonian eel packs a powerful zap, but is it strong enough to vanquish a pack of piranhas? Electric eels paralyze their prey with high-voltage shocks. Pack-hunting piranhas may have small mouths, but their jaws are powerful and their teeth are razor sharp.

RED-BELLIED PIRANHA

This razor-toothed fish has a deadly reputation, but it preys on large animals (or humans) only if they're sick, injured, or already dead.

RED-BELLIED PIRANHA

STATS

5	SPEED
6	STRENGTH
5	BRAINS
8	ATTACK
7	DEFENSE

SCIENTIFIC NAME	*Pygocentrus nattereri*
LENGTH	10–14 inches (25–36 cm)
TYPICAL PREY	Fish, mollusks, insects, crustaceans, carrion, plants
PREDATOR STYLE	Pack hunter, feeds in groups on larger animals
WATER TYPE	Fresh

WHO WINS?
SEE PAGE 110.

GRAY WOLF VS. AFRICAN LEOPARD

GRAY WOLF

The gray wolf is a powerful and intelligent predator. Wolves hunt alone or in packs to bring down large animals. Running at speeds up to 30 mph (48 kph), the wolf separates its prey from the herd and attacks.

SCIENTIFIC NAME	*Canis lupus*
LENGTH (WITHOUT TAIL)	3–5.25 feet (.9–1.6 m)
TYPICAL PREY	Moose, elk, rabbits
PREDATOR STYLE	Stalks and pursues
HABITAT	Canada and the northern United States

GRAY WOLF

STATS

SPEED	7
STRENGTH	7
BRAINS	9
ATTACK	7
DEFENSE	5

THE SHOWDOWN

Here are two beautiful, noble predators. One rules the cold lands of North America, the other sub-Saharan Africa. When a top dog goes up against a cat at the top of its predator game, the fur will fly!

AFRICAN LEOPARD

Strong and graceful, this big cat will often drag its kill—perhaps a 200-pound (90.7-kg) antelope—into a tree to keep it safe from scavengers. The leopard is stealthy and cunning, with powerful legs and a large head.

AFRICAN LEOPARD

STATS

8	SPEED
8	STRENGTH
8	BRAINS
8	ATTACK
7	DEFENSE

SCIENTIFIC NAME	*Panthera pardus pardus*
LENGTH (WITHOUT TAIL)	4.25–6.25 feet (1.3–1.9 m)
TYPICAL PREY	Antelope, deer, pigs
PREDATOR STYLE	Stalks and pounces
HABITAT	Sub-Saharan Africa

WHO WINS?
SEE PAGE 110.

GOLDEN EAGLE VS. GREAT HORNED OWL

GOLDEN EAGLE

One of the largest birds of prey in North America, the golden eagle can kill prey as large as a deer. Able to dive at speeds of up to 150 mph (241 kph), it snatches up small mammals with its sharp talons.

SCIENTIFIC NAME	*Aquila chrysaetos*
TYPICAL SIZE	Body: 33–38 inches (84–97 cm); Wingspan: 7.5 feet (2.3 m)
TYPICAL PREY	Rabbits, squirrels, prairie dogs
PREDATOR STYLE	Flies low to surprise prey
HABITAT	Throughout the Northern Hemisphere

GOLDEN EAGLE

STATS

SPEED	9
STRENGTH	8
BRAINS	4
ATTACK	7
DEFENSE	7

THE SHOWDOWN

The golden eagle and the great horned owl are two noble, evenly matched raptors. Both have huge wingspans and viselike talons. Both can kill prey far larger and heavier than themselves.

GREAT HORNED OWL

This predator hunts at night, attacking from above. When it spots prey, it dives and uses its large, strong talons to kill and then carry away the victim.

GREAT HORNED OWL

STATS

6	SPEED
8	STRENGTH
4	BRAINS
8	ATTACK
7	DEFENSE

SCIENTIFIC NAME	*Bubo virginianus*
TYPICAL SIZE	Body: 18–25 inches (46–64 cm); Wingspan: 3.3–4.8 feet (1–1.5 m)
TYPICAL PREY	Rabbits, mice, geese, other raptors
PREDATOR STYLE	Nighttime hunter; swoops to attack
HABITAT	Common in North and South America

WHO WINS? SEE PAGE 110.

INTO THE DEEP

In the salty habitat of the ocean, the animals, plants, and other life-forms live in different zones.

One way of dividing up the life zones is based on how close the habitat is to shore. Another is based on whether the animals live at the surface, on the sea floor, or in the water column (all the water between the surface and the bottom). Still another is based on how deep the water is and how much light reaches there.

The deep zone, reached by only 1 percent of sunlight or less, is called the aphotic zone. It starts at a depth of about 650 feet (198 m) and goes all the way to the deepest bottom of the ocean.

These are just some of the special weapons used by splashdown predators that live or hunt in the aphotic zone:

GIANT MOUTH

ANGLERFISH

FRILLED SHARK

LURE ON HEAD

ANGLERFISH

LURE ON CHIN

PACIFIC BLACKDRAGON

TRIPLE-SPIKED TEETH

PACIFIC BLACKDRAGON

TENTACLES

GIANT OCTOPUS

GREEN ANACONDA VS. ARAPAIMA

GREEN ANACONDA

Growing as long as a school bus and weighing up to a quarter of a ton (227 kg), the green anaconda is the biggest snake in the world.

SCIENTIFIC NAME	*Eunectes murinus*
LENGTH	20–30 feet (6.1–9.1 m)
TYPICAL PREY	Anything it can catch, including fish, amphibians, reptiles, birds, and mammals
PREDATOR STYLE	Ambush hunter; grabs prey with its teeth, then suffocates it by squeezing
WATER TYPE	Fresh

GREEN ANACONDA

STATS		
SPEED		6
STRENGTH		10
BRAINS	4	
ATTACK		8
DEFENSE		7

THE SPLASHDOWN

The world's biggest snake meets one of the biggest freshwater fish in a contest of Amazonian giants. The green anaconda waits in ambush with only its eyes and nostrils above the water. The arapaima hunts near the surface, sometimes even snatching birds as prey.

ARAPAIMA

This huge fish is an air breather with a primitive lung. The arapaima surfaces about every ten minutes to gulp air with a loud coughing sound.

ARAPAIMA

STATS

7	SPEED
8	STRENGTH
7	BRAINS
7	ATTACK
7	DEFENSE

SCIENTIFIC NAME	*Arapaima gigas*
LENGTH	6–10 feet (1.8–3 m)
TYPICAL PREY	Fish, sometimes birds
PREDATOR STYLE	Hunts near the surface of the water
WATER TYPE	Fresh

WHO WINS?
SEE PAGE 110.

FISHER VS. RED FOX

FISHER

Fishers don't actually eat fish, but they are one of the few animals that hunts porcupines. The fisher is able to stretch out in narrow tunnels to hunt its prey underground. It has retractable claws and is a good tree climber.

SCIENTIFIC NAME	*Martes pennanti*
LENGTH (WITHOUT TAIL)	36 inches (91 cm)
TYPICAL PREY	Rabbits, mice, squirrels, porcupines
PREDATOR STYLE	Active forest hunter; inflicts damage with teeth and claws
HABITAT	Northern mountains of North America

FISHER

STATS		
SPEED		6
STRENGTH		4
BRAINS		5
ATTACK		6
DEFENSE		7

THE SHOWDOWN

The fisher is a relative of the weasel and a fierce predator. The fox is cunning, agile, and fast. Both animals have sharp teeth and claws—and they know how to use them. Who will win in a face-off between these wily fighters?

RED FOX

The red fox uses its keen senses of sight and hearing to track prey such as mice. In fact, a fox can hear a watch ticking up to 40 yards (36.6 m) away!

RED FOX

STATS

7	SPEED	
5	STRENGTH	
7	BRAINS	
5	ATTACK	
6	DEFENSE	

SCIENTIFIC NAME	*Vulpes vulpes*
LENGTH (WITHOUT TAIL)	18–34 inches (46–86 cm)
TYPICAL PREY	Rabbits, mice, birds, fish, frogs
PREDATOR STYLE	Solitary, opportunistic hunter; stalks and pounces
HABITAT	North America, northern Africa, Europe, Asia

WHO WINS?
SEE PAGE 110.

SPERM WHALE VS. GIANT SQUID

SPERM WHALE

This bus-sized whale is the biggest toothed predator on Earth. Sperm whales can dive deeper than a mile (1.6 km) and hold their breath for an hour and a half.

SCIENTIFIC NAME	*Physeter macrocephalus*
LENGTH	25–50 feet (7.6–15.2 m)
TYPICAL PREY	Squid and octopuses
PREDATOR STYLE	Dives as deep as 0.6 miles (1 km) or more in pursuit of squid; probably uses echolocation (sonar) to find prey
WATER TYPE	Salt

SPERM WHALE

STATS		
SPEED	8
STRENGTH		10
BRAINS	8
ATTACK	8
DEFENSE	7

THE SPLASHDOWN

Ancient opponents face off far below the surface in this deep-sea splashdown. Sperm whales' favorite prey is squid, but the tentacle scars on many whales' heads are proof that the giant squid can hold its own in a fight.

GIANT SQUID

This deep-sea giant's basketball-sized eyes are the largest in the animal kingdom. Before 2004, no one had ever taken a picture of a living giant squid.

GIANT SQUID

STATS

SPEED	6
STRENGTH	9
BRAINS	6
ATTACK	8
DEFENSE	9

SCIENTIFIC NAME	*Architeuthis dux*
LENGTH	10–40 feet (3–12.2 m)
TYPICAL PREY	Deep-sea fish, smaller squid
PREDATOR STYLE	Grabs prey with its two club-tipped tentacles, then drags it within reach of eight arms and a parrot-like beak
WATER TYPE	Salt

WHO WINS?
SEE PAGE 110.

STOAT VS. YELLOW MONGOOSE

STOAT

The stoat is a wily predator. It has a good sense of smell, which it uses to track its prey. It climbs trees to go after birds and steal their eggs. Its jaws and sharp teeth kill with a quick bite.

SCIENTIFIC NAME	*Mustela erminea*
LENGTH (WITHOUT TAIL)	12 inches (30 cm)
TYPICAL PREY	Mice, insects, rabbits
PREDATOR STYLE	Opportunistic; takes whatever it can get its paws on
HABITAT	United Kingdom and northern Europe

STOAT

STATS

SPEED	6
STRENGTH	4
BRAINS	4
ATTACK	4
DEFENSE	4

THE SHOWDOWN

The stoat and the mongoose look alike, but they are not related. Both are fast and equipped with sharp teeth and claws. Is one more aggressive? If so, that might give it the winning edge.

YELLOW MONGOOSE

The mongoose is a famous snake killer. It is quick enough to avoid the snake when it strikes and keeps dodging until the snake is exhausted. Then the mongoose bites the snake, breaking its spine and crushing its head.

YELLOW MONGOOSE

STATS

7	SPEED
4	STRENGTH
4	BRAINS
5	ATTACK
4	DEFENSE

SCIENTIFIC NAME	*Cynictis penicillata*
LENGTH (WITHOUT TAIL)	9–13 inches (23–33 cm)
TYPICAL PREY	Snakes, mice, insects, birds
PREDATOR STYLE	Quick attack and strong bite
HABITAT	Southern Africa

WHO WINS? SEE PAGE 110.

GIANT MORAY VS. LONGFIN EEL

GIANT MORAY

One of the biggest moray eels, the giant moray prowls for prey among the cracks and crevices of its coral-reef home. It will attack humans if threatened.

SCIENTIFIC NAME	*Gymnothorax javanicus*
LENGTH	Up to 10 feet (3 m)
TYPICAL PREY	Fish, crustaceans
PREDATOR STYLE	Hunts in coral reefs
WATER TYPE	Salt

GIANT MORAY

STATS

SPEED	5
STRENGTH	5
BRAINS	5
ATTACK	5
DEFENSE	5

THE SPLASHDOWN

It's every eel for itself when the saltwater moray meets the river-dwelling longfin. The giant moray lives in shallow-water ocean reefs. The longfin eel spends its whole life in fresh water, then swims downstream to the ocean to spawn.

LONGFIN EEL

This eel has a long life to match its long body. Some New Zealand longfin eels live more than 100 years.

LONGFIN EEL

STATS

5	SPEED
4	STRENGTH
3	BRAINS
3	ATTACK
3	DEFENSE

SCIENTIFIC NAME	*Anguilla dieffenbachii*
LENGTH	2–5 feet (61–152 cm)
TYPICAL PREY	Fish, crustaceans
PREDATOR STYLE	Stalks prey among rocks and plants on river and lake bottoms
WATER TYPE	Fresh

WHO WINS?
SEE PAGE 110.

GREAT HAMMERHEAD VS. LEMON SHARK

GREAT HAMMERHEAD

Like other sharks, the great hammerhead has electricity-sensing organs in its head for detecting prey. The wide head shape spreads these organs out for better sensitivity.

SCIENTIFIC NAME	*Sphyrna mokarran*
LENGTH	10–20 feet (3–6.1 m)
TYPICAL PREY	Fish, especially rays and skates
PREDATOR STYLE	Hunts along the sea floor using special electricity-sensing organs to detect stingrays and other bottom fish
WATER TYPE	Salt

GREAT HAMMERHEAD

STATS

SPEED	7
STRENGTH	9
BRAINS	5
ATTACK	9
DEFENSE	9

THE SPLASHDOWN

The largest of the hammerhead sharks, the great hammerhead sometimes preys on young lemon sharks. But at more than 10 feet (3 m) long, a full-grown lemon shark is a different story. Who will prove toughest in this shark-to-shark splashdown?

LEMON SHARK

This shark gets its name from its yellow-brown color. Lemon sharks live in coastal waters of North and South America, as well as West Africa.

LEMON SHARK

STATS

7	SPEED	
9	STRENGTH	
5	BRAINS	
8	ATTACK	
8	DEFENSE	

SCIENTIFIC NAME	*Negaprion brevirostris*
LENGTH	8–11 feet (2.4–3.4 m)
TYPICAL PREY	Fish, crabs, crayfish, sometimes seabirds
PREDATOR STYLE	Stalks prey near the sea floor in shallow areas
WATER TYPE	Salt

WHO WINS?
SEE PAGE 110.

GRASSLAND PREDATORS

Grasslands are wetter than deserts, but the yearly dry seasons in these habitats mean there's not enough water year-round for forests to grow.

Savannas are grasslands with widely spaced trees. They're found in tropical parts of the world with warm or hot climates. Savannas have a rainy season and a dry season with hardly any rain at all. Africa, South America, India, and Australia all have large savanna areas.

Prairies, plains, veldts, and steppes are grasslands with hardly any trees. They're found in temperate zones, the areas north and south of the tropics where there are hot summers and cold winters. Temperate grasslands cover large areas in North America, South America, Central Asia, and southern Africa.

These are some of the special weapons used by predators of the grasslands:

SUPER SPEED

CHEETAH

POWERFUL DIVE

PEREGRINE FALCON

GRASPING CLAWS

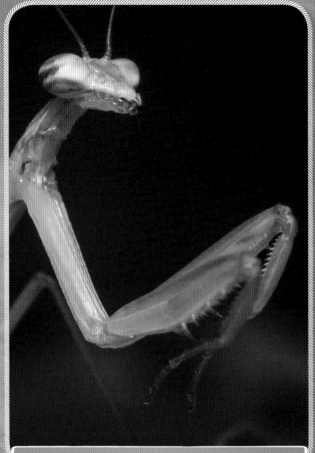

CHINESE PRAYING MANTIS

POWERFUL JAWS

LION

VENOMOUS FANGS

PUFF ADDER

FANG-DODGING AGILITY

MONGOOSE

TASMANIAN DEVIL VS. DINGO

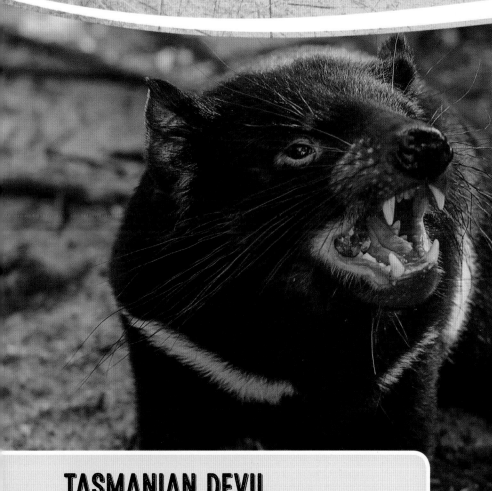

TASMANIAN DEVIL

The Tasmanian devil is known for impressive displays of ferocity—baring its teeth, lunging, screeching, and growling. In size and shape, these dangerous mammals look a bit like baby bears, but don't let these cuddly bundles of fur fool you.

SCIENTIFIC NAME	*Sarcophilus harrisii*
LENGTH (WITHOUT TAIL)	1.7–2.6 feet (.5–.8 m)
TYPICAL PREY	Snakes, birds, fish, carrion
PREDATOR STYLE	Ambush, power; jaws crush bones and all of prey eaten
HABITAT	The island of Tasmania, off Australia

TASMANIAN DEVIL

STATS

SPEED	5
STRENGTH	5
BRAINS	4
ATTACK	7
DEFENSE	6

THE SHOWDOWN

The intelligent dingo goes up against the Tasmanian devil, with its reputation for unpredictable behavior. The dingo's jaws are bigger, but the Tasmanian devil's jaws exert more force, pound for pound, than those of any other mammal in the world.

DINGO

This predator uses its smarts to survive in the harsh environment of its native Australia. Dingoes generally hunt for rabbits, rodents, birds, and lizards, but in a pack, they can bring down an animal as large and powerful as a kangaroo.

DINGO

STATS

8	SPEED	
	5	STRENGTH
8	BRAINS	
	5	ATTACK
	4	DEFENSE

SCIENTIFIC NAME	*Canis lupus dingo*
LENGTH (WITHOUT TAIL)	3.5–4 feet (1.1–1.2 m)
TYPICAL PREY	Rabbits, birds, rodents, lizards
PREDATOR STYLE	Like wolf cousins, the dingo stalks its prey; uses stamina to chase and pounce
HABITAT	Australia (not Tasmania) and Southeast Asia

WHO WINS?
SEE PAGE 110.

BLUE MARLIN VS. SWORDFISH

BLUE MARLIN

Famous as a fighter, the blue marlin is the biggest of the billfishes. Large females can weigh in at nearly 1 ton (907 kg).

SCIENTIFIC NAME	*Makaira nigricans*
LENGTH	7–16 feet (2.1–4.9 m)
TYPICAL PREY	Open-ocean fish such as tuna, mackerel, and dolphinfish (mahimahi)
PREDATOR STYLE	Swims right into schools of fish to attack, may stun prey with quick sideways slashes of its bill
WATER TYPE	Salt

BLUE MARLIN

STATS

SPEED	10
STRENGTH	9
BRAINS	6
ATTACK	7
DEFENSE	8

THE SPLASHDOWN

This splashdown pits two powerful members of the billfish family against each other. These open-ocean predators may look as if they're about to cross swords, but they don't use these bills as stabbing weapons. The bill is an extension of the upper jaw.

SWORDFISH

Swordfish can dive deeper than 2,000 feet (610 m) in pursuit of prey. This fish is one of the fastest swimmers in the ocean.

SWORDFISH

STATS

10	SPEED	
9	STRENGTH	
6	BRAINS	
7	ATTACK	
7	DEFENSE	

SCIENTIFIC NAME	*Xiphias gladius*
LENGTH	5–14.5 feet (1.5–4.4 m)
TYPICAL PREY	Open-ocean fish of all types, sometimes squid or cuttlefish
PREDATOR STYLE	Slashes with its bill to stun, kill, or knock prey out of a school of fish
WATER TYPE	Salt

WHO WINS?
SEE PAGE 110.

PLATYPUS VS. REEF NEEDLEFISH

PLATYPUS

The platypus is one of only two mammal types that lays eggs. Its body is built for swimming and digging in muddy lake and river bottoms.

SCIENTIFIC NAME	*Ornithorhynchus anatinus*
LENGTH	12–24 inches (30–61 cm)
TYPICAL PREY	Insects, mollusks, worms
PREDATOR STYLE	Forages for prey on river bottoms
WATER TYPE	Fresh

PLATYPUS

STATS

SPEED	4
STRENGTH	4
BRAINS	6
ATTACK	1
DEFENSE	7

THE SPLASHDOWN

A freshwater mammal meets a saltwater fish in this contest between two strange-looking predators. Male platypuses defend themselves with venomous spurs on their hind legs. Needlefish beaks are needle sharp and can cause serious injury.

REEF NEEDLEFISH

These needlefish often make high-speed leaps out of the water as they swim near the surface. Humans have been injured and even killed by flying needlefish.

REEF NEEDLEFISH

STATS

9	SPEED	
5	STRENGTH	
4	BRAINS	
2	ATTACK	
6	DEFENSE	

SCIENTIFIC NAME	*Strongylura incisa*
LENGTH	24–39 inches (61–99 cm)
TYPICAL PREY	Fish
PREDATOR STYLE	Hunts near the surface; uses jaws to snap up fish, does not use its beak to spear prey
WATER TYPE	Salt

WHO WINS?
SEE PAGE 110.

RETICULATED PYTHON VS. KING COBRA

RETICULATED PYTHON

Reticulated pythons are constrictors. Although they are not venomous, pythons can deliver vicious bites with their sharp, curved teeth—100 in all!

SCIENTIFIC NAME	*Python reticulatus*
LENGTH	10–20 feet (3–6 m)
TYPICAL PREY	Rodents, wild boar, deer
PREDATOR STYLE	Ambush, constricting coils
HABITAT	Southeast Asia and nearby islands

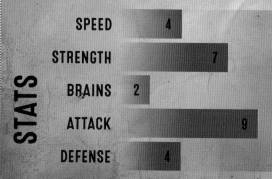

RETICULATED PYTHON

STATS

SPEED	4
STRENGTH	7
BRAINS	2
ATTACK	9
DEFENSE	4

THE SHOWDOWN

The longest snake in the world vs. the largest venomous snake. Each is known for its strength, speed, and cunning. But while the reticulated python has size on its side, the king cobra is known as the "snake eater" for a reason.

KING COBRA

Although they don't have the strongest venom, king cobras can deliver enough in a single bite to kill 20 people. King cobras can attack as far as they can raise their bodies; for an adult cobra, this yields a strike zone of up to 5 feet (1.5 m).

KING COBRA

STATS

7	SPEED	
5	STRENGTH	
4	BRAINS	
7	ATTACK	
5	DEFENSE	

SCIENTIFIC NAME	*Ophiophagus hannah*
LENGTH	13 feet (4 m)
TYPICAL PREY	Snakes, lizards, small mammals
PREDATOR STYLE	Quick attack, venomous bite
HABITAT	Rain forests and plains of India, southern China, and Southeast Asia

WHO WINS?
SEE PAGE 111.

PEREGRINE FALCON VS. BOBCAT

PEREGRINE FALCON

The fastest-flying birds in the world, peregrine falcons can reach diving speeds of 200 mph (322 kph). They snag prey in midair with their talons.

SCIENTIFIC NAME	*Falco peregrinus*
TYPICAL SIZE	Body: 14–19 inches (36–48 cm); Wingspan: 3.5 feet (1 m)
TYPICAL PREY	Starlings, pigeons, bats
PREDATOR STYLE	Pursuit; high-speed dive to capture prey
HABITAT	Throughout the world, except Antarctica

PEREGRINE FALCON

STATS

SPEED	10
STRENGTH	4
BRAINS	5
ATTACK	6
DEFENSE	3

THE SHOWDOWN

Cat against bird. Usually the cat would win, but the peregrine falcon has the advantage of terrific diving speed, strong talons, and a vicious hooked beak. The bobcat, on the other hand, is agile and able to leap as far as 10 feet (3 m) to pounce.

BOBCAT

These elusive nocturnal creatures are about twice the size of a house cat. The bobcat hunts by stalking prey from under cover and pouncing on it when the prey wanders close.

BOBCAT

STATS

7	SPEED
8	STRENGTH
7	BRAINS
7	ATTACK
6	DEFENSE

SCIENTIFIC NAME	*Lynx rufus*
TYPICAL SIZE	26–41 inches (66–104 cm) long, not including tail
TYPICAL PREY	Rabbits, birds, mice, squirrels
PREDATOR STYLE	Stealth; leaps and pounces
WATER TYPE	Southern Canada, United States, and northern Mexico

WHO WINS?
SEE PAGE 111.

BLUEFIN TUNA

These huge, fast-swimming fish travel long distances across the ocean in schools. Unlike most fish, they are endothermic (warm-blooded) and create their own body heat.

SCIENTIFIC NAME	*Thunnus thynnus*
LENGTH	6–9.75 feet (1.8–3 m)
TYPICAL PREY	Smaller fish of all types, squid, crustaceans
PREDATOR STYLE	Sprints with bursts of speed to chase fast schools of fish; cruises along with its mouth open to gulp down slower-moving prey
WATER TYPE	Salt

BLUEFIN TUNA

STATS

SPEED	10
STRENGTH	8
BRAINS	5
ATTACK	5
DEFENSE	5

THE SPLASHDOWN

These two predators will probably never meet in the real world, but with the invasive lionfish spreading through North American waters, it's not impossible. Can the lionfish's venomous spines stand up to the tuna's vastly superior size?

RED LIONFISH

The venomous spines on this fish's back are for defense, not hunting. But lionfish are aggressive and may threaten or attack with their spines facing forward.

RED LIONFISH

STATS		
3	SPEED	
3	STRENGTH	
3	BRAINS	
3	ATTACK	
9	DEFENSE	

SCIENTIFIC NAME	*Pterois volitans*
LENGTH	12–15 inches (30–38 cm)
TYPICAL PREY	Crabs, shrimp, small fish
PREDATOR STYLE	Stalks, then strikes when the prey is cornered and swallows it whole
WATER TYPE	Salt

WHO WINS?
SEE PAGE 111.

BULLET ANT VS. ASSASSIN BUG

BULLET ANT

This tiny predator is named for its painful sting, and it will attack if its nest is threatened. The ants swarm out, grab the intruders, and impale them with their retractable stingers.

SCIENTIFIC NAME	*Paraponera clavata*
LENGTH	1 inch (2.5 cm)
TYPICAL PREY	Termites and other insects
PREDATOR STYLE	Patrols and attacks
HABITAT	Central and South America

BULLET ANT

STATS		
SPEED		8
STRENGTH		9
BRAINS	5	
ATTACK	7	
DEFENSE	7	

THE SHOWDOWN

These two predators have fierce stings, and they're not afraid to use them. The assassin bug is an ambush hunter, while the bullet ant goes out in search of prey. The question: Which insect would strike first?

ASSASSIN BUG

Assassin bugs are called that because they are masters of the surprise attack. They lie in wait for their prey, quickly stab the victim, and then inject it with lethal venom.

ASSASSIN BUG

STATS

8	SPEED
5	STRENGTH
3	BRAINS
8	ATTACK
5	DEFENSE

SCIENTIFIC NAME	*Rasahus hamatus*
LENGTH	1 inch (2.5 cm)
TYPICAL PREY	Caterpillars and other insects, small mammals
PREDATOR STYLE	Stalks and strikes
HABITAT	Varieties throughout the world

WHO WINS?
SEE PAGE 111.

THE UPPER OCEAN

The ocean's upper life zone, where there is enough sunlight for plants and algae, is called the photic zone. This zone goes from the surface down to about 650 feet (198 m). Photic-zone predators include animals that live near the surface, in the water column, or on the sea bottom.

These are some of the special weapons used by splashdown predators that live or hunt at least some of the time in the photic zone:

VENOMOUS BITE

BANDED SEA KRAIT

VENOMOUS SPINES

LIONFISH

ELECTRIC SHOCK

ELECTRIC RAY

TEETH

GREAT WHITE SHARK

VENOMOUS STING

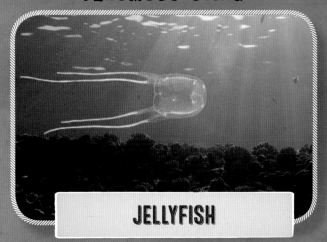

JELLYFISH

CLAWS

POLAR BEAR

NORTHERN STARGAZER

The stargazer's upward-staring eyes let it watch for prey while buried in the sand. This fish defends itself with an electric shock of up to 50 volts.

SCIENTIFIC NAME	*Astroscopus guttatus*
LENGTH	8–22 inches (20–56 cm)
TYPICAL PREY	Any small fish that swim close enough
PREDATOR STYLE	Hides under the sand, then pops up to swallow prey whole
WATER TYPE	Salt

NORTHERN STARGAZER

STATS

SPEED	2
STRENGTH	2
BRAINS	3
ATTACK	3
DEFENSE	5

THE SPLASHDOWN

East meets west as two ocean-bottom predators try to out-zap each other in this electrifying contest. The stargazer and electric ray live on opposite coasts of North America. Both predators can zing their enemies with an electric shock.

PACIFIC ELECTRIC RAY

This electrifying predator can zap an attacker with a 50-volt jolt, enough to knock a human down. It also uses its electricity to subdue prey.

PACIFIC ELECTRIC RAY

STATS

4	SPEED
4	STRENGTH
4	BRAINS
5	ATTACK
5	DEFENSE

SCIENTIFIC NAME	*Torpedo californica*
LENGTH	2–4.5 feet (61–137 cm)
TYPICAL PREY	Fish
PREDATOR STYLE	Hunts by swimming in the water column at night and by ambush on the sea floor during the day; subdues prey with electric shocks
WATER TYPE	Salt

WHO WINS?
SEE PAGE 111.

LION VS. SPOTTED HYENA

LION

The second-largest felines (only tigers are bigger), lions are apex predators of the savannas. Lions chase away intruders with intimidating roars. They have powerful legs and canine teeth that are 3 inches (8 cm) long.

SCIENTIFIC NAME	*Panthera leo*
LENGTH (WITHOUT TAIL)	4.5–6.5 feet (1.4–2 m)
TYPICAL PREY	Wildebeest, impala, zebra, buffalo
PREDATOR STYLE	Stalks, rushes; strangles victims with bite to the neck
HABITAT	Sub-Saharan Africa; Gir Forest in India

LION

STATS		
SPEED	4	
STRENGTH	5	
BRAINS		8
ATTACK		8
DEFENSE	4	

THE SHOWDOWN

Lions and hyenas are sworn enemies. Male lions routinely steal hyenas' kill. Hyenas chase female lions and steal their kill. Hyenas also kill and eat sick or injured lions. But when the two face off, who will come out on top—the king of the beasts or the maniacal laughing hyena?

SPOTTED HYENA

These skillful hunters use their strong jaws to chomp through skin and bone. Although they can hang on to a moving animal with their jaws, they do not have a killing bite.

SPOTTED HYENA

STATS

7	SPEED	
7	STRENGTH	
6	BRAINS	
7	ATTACK	
4	DEFENSE	

SCIENTIFIC NAME	*Crocuta crocuta*
LENGTH (WITHOUT TAIL)	3–5 feet (.9–1.5 m)
TYPICAL PREY	Wildebeest and zebra are favorites but will scavenge anything
PREDATOR STYLE	Persistence; runs prey to exhaustion
HABITAT	Throughout much of Africa, the Arabian Peninsula, and India

WHO WINS?
SEE PAGE 111.

BANDED SEA KRAIT VS. SEA SNAKE

BANDED SEA KRAIT

This snake hunts eels in the crevices of coral reefs. With its round body and paddle-like tail, it's equally at home on land and in the water.

SCIENTIFIC NAME	*Laticauda colubrina*
LENGTH	2.5–4 feet (76–122 cm)
TYPICAL PREY	Eels
PREDATOR STYLE	Hunts eels in coral reefs; subdues them with its venomous bite
WATER TYPE	Salt

BANDED SEA KRAIT

STATS		
SPEED	4	
STRENGTH	4	
BRAINS	4	
ATTACK		7
DEFENSE		7

THE SPLASHDOWN

A head-to-head match between two venomous seagoing snakes! The banded sea krait hunts and feeds in water but goes on land to rest, nest, and lay eggs. The yellow-bellied sea snake spends its entire life at sea.

YELLOW-BELLIED SEA SNAKE

This snake can stay underwater for up to three hours. Its narrow flattened body makes it an expert swimmer, but it can't crawl on land.

SEA SNAKE

STATS

4	SPEED
4	STRENGTH
4	BRAINS
7	ATTACK
7	DEFENSE

SCIENTIFIC NAME	*Pelamis platurus*
LENGTH	1–3.5 feet (30–107 cm)
TYPICAL PREY	Fish
PREDATOR STYLE	Floats on the surface to ambush fish as they swim up underneath
WATER TYPE	Salt

WHO WINS?
SEE PAGE 111.

RABID WOLF SPIDER VS. BLACK WIDOW

RABID WOLF SPIDER

This spider gets its name because of its wolflike hunting strategy: it stalks its prey, then charges in to attack. Also, it is not afraid to assault a creature much larger than itself.

SCIENTIFIC NAME	*Rabidosa rabida*
LENGTH (WITHOUT LEGS)	Female: 1 inch (2.5 cm)
TYPICAL PREY	Insects
PREDATOR STYLE	Stalks and chases prey
HABITAT	Central and eastern North America

RABID WOLF SPIDER

STATS

SPEED	5
STRENGTH	5
BRAINS	3
ATTACK	8
DEFENSE	6

THE SHOWDOWN

Two small but creepy predators battle it out. The wolf spider is an ambush hunter, lying in wait for prey. The black widow traps prey in its web and then administers a lethal bite.

BLACK WIDOW

The black widow is the most venomous spider in North America. When the black widow senses prey in its web, it comes out of hiding, bites the victim, injects venom, and holds it with its legs until it stops struggling.

BLACK WIDOW

STATS

5	SPEED	
4	STRENGTH	
2	BRAINS	
6	ATTACK	
8	DEFENSE	

SCIENTIFIC NAME	*Latrodectus mactans*
LENGTH (WITHOUT LEGS)	Female: .5 inch (1.3 cm)
TYPICAL PREY	Insects
PREDATOR STYLE	Attacks insects caught in web
HABITAT	Throughout much of the United States and southern Canada

WHO WINS? SEE PAGE 111.

GIANT PACIFIC OCTOPUS VS. HARBOR SEAL

GIANT PACIFIC OCTOPUS

This giant is a master of camouflage, changing color to blend in with its surroundings. Its soft body also lets it squeeze into very small hiding places.

SCIENTIFIC NAME	*Enteroctopus dofleini*
LENGTH	9–16 feet (2.7–4.9 m)
TYPICAL PREY	Crabs, clams, snails, fish, and anything else it can catch
PREDATOR STYLE	Waits in ambush, then grabs prey with sucker-covered arms and paralyzes it with a venomous bite
WATER TYPE	Salt

GIANT PACIFIC OCTOPUS

STATS

SPEED	5
STRENGTH	8
BRAINS	9
ATTACK	6
DEFENSE	6

THE SPLASHDOWN

It's mollusk against mammal as the world's largest octopus meets the swift-swimming harbor seal. Octopuses are sometimes on the seal's dinner menu, but this one's a bit different: its arms can spread wider than the length of a minivan!

HARBOR SEAL

This hunter can hold its breath for more than 20 minutes and dive as deep as 650 feet (198 m), but most hunting dives are shorter and shallower.

HARBOR SEAL

STATS

7	SPEED	
7	STRENGTH	
8	BRAINS	
6	ATTACK	
6	DEFENSE	

SCIENTIFIC NAME	*Phoca vitulina*
LENGTH	5–6 feet (1.5–1.8 m)
TYPICAL PREY	Fish, octopuses, squid, crabs, shrimp
PREDATOR STYLE	Chases schools of fish, dives to sea bottom for octopuses, crabs, and shrimp
WATER TYPE	Salt

WHO WINS?
SEE PAGE 111.

OSPREY VS. BALD EAGLE

OSPREY

From as high as 100 feet (30 m) in the sky, the osprey sees a fish and dives. It grips the fish with its claws and pulls it from the water. The osprey has to be powerful to drag a big, slippery fish to the surface.

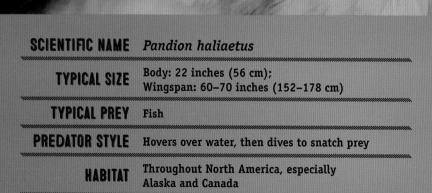

SCIENTIFIC NAME	*Pandion haliaetus*
TYPICAL SIZE	Body: 22 inches (56 cm); Wingspan: 60–70 inches (152–178 cm)
TYPICAL PREY	Fish
PREDATOR STYLE	Hovers over water, then dives to snatch prey
HABITAT	Throughout North America, especially Alaska and Canada

OSPREY

STATS

SPEED	8
STRENGTH	6
BRAINS	5
ATTACK	5
DEFENSE	4

THE SHOWDOWN

These two birds of prey inhabit many of the same regions and occasionally fight over prey. The bald eagle is definitely bigger, but the osprey is a faster flier and is more agile in the air.

BALD EAGLE

The bald eagle holds its wings out flat as it soars overhead in large looping circles and uses its sharp eyes to watch for prey. When it sees prey, it swoops down and uses sharp talons to grab its victim.

BALD EAGLE

STATS

7	SPEED
7	STRENGTH
5	BRAINS
7	ATTACK
6	DEFENSE

SCIENTIFIC NAME	*Haliaeetus leucocephalus*
TYPICAL SIZE	Body: 32 inches (81 cm); Wingspan: 80 inches (203 cm)
TYPICAL PREY	Fish, large birds, mammals
PREDATOR STYLE	Swoops down to grab fish from stream or bay; will steal other animals' kills
HABITAT	North America

WHO WINS? SEE PAGE 111.

BALLOONFISH VS. OYSTER TOADFISH

BALLOONFISH

When threatened, this fish inflates itself with water until it is almost completely spherical. Sharp spines stick out of its body to keep attackers at bay.

SCIENTIFIC NAME	*Diodon holocanthus*
LENGTH	8–20 inches (20–51 cm)
TYPICAL PREY	Snails, sea urchins, hermit crabs
PREDATOR STYLE	Hunts at night along the ocean floor
WATER TYPE	Salt

BALLOONFISH

STATS		
SPEED	3	
STRENGTH	2	
BRAINS		4
ATTACK	1	
DEFENSE		6

THE SPLASHDOWN

The prickly balloonfish meets the warty-looking toadfish in a contest of shell-crunching mollusk-eaters. Both of these bottom dwellers subdue their prey with powerful jaws and crushing teeth. But can the toadfish get past the balloonfish's prickly spines?

OYSTER TOADFISH

This fish defends itself with snapping jaws and a spiny dorsal (back) fin. During mating season, males call to females with a booming, foghorn-like voice.

OYSTER TOADFISH

STATS

3	SPEED	
3	STRENGTH	
3	BRAINS	
2	ATTACK	
9	DEFENSE	

SCIENTIFIC NAME	*Opsanus tau*
LENGTH	Up to 12 inches (30 cm)
TYPICAL PREY	Mollusks, crustaceans, small fish, squid
PREDATOR STYLE	Snaps up prey with its powerful jaws
WATER TYPE	Salt

WHO WINS?
SEE PAGE 111.

FOREST PREDATORS

Forests are where the trees are. There are different types, depending on where they are in the world and what kinds of trees grow there.

Tropical forests grow in the tropics, the areas close to the equator. Temperatures there change very little during the year, so instead of four seasons, these forest habitats have just two: wet and dry. Or sometimes just one: wet. Tropical forests include rain forests, cloud forests (high in the mountains), and monsoon forests, which have the longest dry seasons.

Temperate forests grow in the areas north of the equator where there are four separate seasons, with warm summers and cold winters. Some have deciduous (dih-SIH-joo-uhs) trees, or trees with leaves that fall off in the autumn. Others have conifers, or trees with cones and needles. Still others have both types of trees.

Boreal forests grow in the far north of Europe, Asia, and North America. These conifer forests are also called taiga.

Here are some of the special weapons used by fierce fighters of the forest:

CONSTRICTING COILS

RETICULATED PYTHON

INTELLIGENCE & COOPERATION

GRAY WOLF

SUPER STEALTH

MOUNTAIN LION

KNIFELIKE CLAWS

GRIZZLY BEAR

VENOMOUS STING

ASIAN GIANT HORNET

VENOMOUS BITE

RABID WOLF SPIDER

GIANT OTTER VS. STINGRAY

GIANT OTTER

Giant otters live and often hunt together in family groups. This member of the weasel family can weigh in at as much as 75 lb (34 kg).

SCIENTIFIC NAME	*Pteronura brasiliensis*
LENGTH	5–6 feet (1.5–1.8 m)
TYPICAL PREY	Fish
PREDATOR STYLE	Hunts alone or in groups in the water near the banks of rivers, streams, and lakes
WATER TYPE	Fresh

GIANT OTTER

STATS		
SPEED	6	
STRENGTH	6	
BRAINS		8
ATTACK	7	
DEFENSE	7	

THE SPLASHDOWN

It's a South American splashdown as the world's longest otter faces off against a small, river-dwelling stingray. The otter is more than five times the size of the stingray, but the ray has a powerful secret weapon: its venomous sting!

SMOOTH-BACKED FRESHWATER STINGRAY

Like its saltwater cousins, this river-dwelling stingray defends itself with a barbed, venom-tipped spine near the base of its tail. The sting is painful but not deadly.

STINGRAY

STATS

5	SPEED	
3	STRENGTH	
4	BRAINS	
3	ATTACK	
7	DEFENSE	

SCIENTIFIC NAME	*Potamotrygon orbignyi*
LENGTH	9–15 inches (23–38 cm)
TYPICAL PREY	Water-dwelling insects and crustaceans
PREDATOR STYLE	Uses special sensor cells around its mouth to detect electrical charges from prey along the river bottom
WATER TYPE	Fresh

WHO WINS?
SEE PAGE 111.

SERVAL VS. CHEETAH

SERVAL

The serval uses its excellent hearing to locate prey—it can even hear animals in their burrows underground. When the serval finds an animal, it leaps high into the air and pounces with enough force to stun the prey.

SCIENTIFIC NAME	*Felis serval*
LENGTH (WITHOUT TAIL)	3 feet (.9 m)
TYPICAL PREY	Antelope, birds, hares, frogs, fish
PREDATOR STYLE	Stalks, leaps, and pounces
HABITAT	Found in most parts of Africa

STATS

SERVAL

SPEED	7
STRENGTH	6
BRAINS	7
ATTACK	8
DEFENSE	6

THE SHOWDOWN

The serval and the cheetah are great hunters of the African savannas. The serval is the most successful hunter of the cat family because of its sharp sense of hearing and ability to pounce. The cheetah is strong and agile; it uses its tail as a rudder to help it turn midsprint.

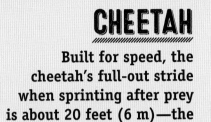

CHEETAH

Built for speed, the cheetah's full-out stride when sprinting after prey is about 20 feet (6 m)—the same as that of a racehorse. When the cheetah catches its prey, it holds it by the neck to strangle it.

CHEETAH

STATS

9		SPEED
	7	STRENGTH
	7	BRAINS
	7	ATTACK
	7	DEFENSE

SCIENTIFIC NAME	*Acinonyx jubatus*
LENGTH (WITHOUT TAIL)	4 feet (1.2 m)
TYPICAL PREY	Antelope, birds, rabbits
PREDATOR STYLE	Stalks and sprints after prey
HABITAT	Central and southern Africa

WHO WINS?
SEE PAGE 111.

ANGLERFISH VS. PELICAN EEL

HUMPBACK ANGLERFISH

Also known as the black seadevil, this deep-ocean dweller attracts prey to its doom with a glowing lure. The lure's blue glow comes from light-emitting bacteria.

SCIENTIFIC NAME	*Melanocetus johnsonii*
LENGTH	Up to 7 inches (18 cm)
TYPICAL PREY	Deep-sea fish
PREDATOR STYLE	Attracts prey with glowing lure at the end of its "fishing rod"
WATER TYPE	Salt

ANGLERFISH

STATS

SPEED	2
STRENGTH	2
BRAINS	2
ATTACK	5
DEFENSE	5

THE SPLASHDOWN

Two bizarre-looking predators meet in the complete darkness of the deepest ocean. Both of these fish have bioluminescent (living, light-producing) organs that glow in the dark. These glowing lures attract prey in a world where animals are few and far between.

PELICAN EEL

This predator's huge mouth opens enough to gulp down prey wider than the eel itself. Its tail has a pink-glowing tip that may act as a lure.

PELICAN EEL

STATS

2	SPEED
2	STRENGTH
2	BRAINS
2	ATTACK
2	DEFENSE

SCIENTIFIC NAME	*Eurypharynx pelecanoides*
LENGTH	Up to 30 inches (76 cm)
TYPICAL PREY	Fish, crustaceans, squid
PREDATOR STYLE	Lunges and gulps prey down with its enormous mouth
WATER TYPE	Salt

WHO WINS?
SEE PAGE 111.

PORTUGUESE MAN-OF-WAR VS. BOX JELLYFISH

PORTUGUESE MAN-OF-WAR

This "predator" is made up of individual, smaller animals called polyps. Four different types of polyps form the float, tendrils, and digestive and reproductive systems.

SCIENTIFIC NAME	*Physalia physalis*
LENGTH	Its float is only 12 inches (30 cm), but its tendrils can extend 30–165 feet (9–50 m)
TYPICAL PREY	Small fish and fish larvae, squid
PREDATOR STYLE	Drifts with wind and current, stings prey that gets caught in its tendrils
WATER TYPE	Salt

PORTUGUESE MAN-OF-WAR

STATS		
SPEED	1
STRENGTH	1
BRAINS	1
ATTACK	8
DEFENSE	8

THE SPLASHDOWN

Two venomous predators go tentacle-to-tentacle in this contest. The Portuguese man-of-war is actually a colony of animals that join together to form a jellyfish-like structure. The box jellyfish is a single, deadly animal. Both hunt by stinging their prey with powerful toxins.

AUSTRALIAN BOX JELLYFISH

The box jellyfish is one of the deadliest animals in the world. Its tentacles sting with powerful venom that can be fatal to even large animals and humans.

BOX JELLYFISH

STATS

1	SPEED
1	STRENGTH
1	BRAINS
10	ATTACK
10	DEFENSE

SCIENTIFIC NAME	*Chironex fleckeri*
LENGTH	Tentacles as long as 10 feet (3 m), with a 12-inch (30-cm) bell
TYPICAL PREY	Fish, shrimp
PREDATOR STYLE	Propels itself through the water, stings prey that gets caught in its tentacles
WATER TYPE	Salt

WHO WINS?
SEE PAGE 111.

PACIFIC BLACKDRAGON VS. FRILLED SHARK

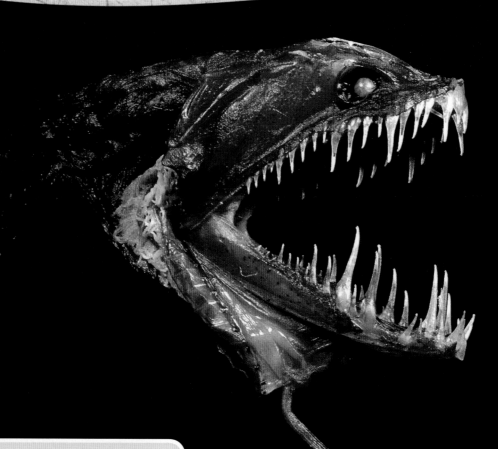

PACIFIC BLACKDRAGON

This deep-sea fish swims up to shallower waters at night to feed. Its long "chin whisker," called a barbel, may act as a lure to attract prey.

SCIENTIFIC NAME	*Idiacanthus antrostomus*
LENGTH	Up to 2 feet (61 cm)
TYPICAL PREY	Crustaceans, small fish
PREDATOR STYLE	Swims closer to the surface at night to feed, then returns to the lower depths during the day; may attract prey with its dangling lure
WATER TYPE	Salt

PACIFIC BLACKDRAGON

STATS

SPEED	2
STRENGTH	3
BRAINS	2
ATTACK	3
DEFENSE	3

THE SPLASHDOWN

This deep-sea splashdown may look like a mismatch between the fang-mouthed blackdragon and the much larger frilled shark, but size isn't everything. Speed counts, too, and the blackdragon may be faster. Scientists don't know much about these mysterious fishes' hunting behavior.

FRILLED SHARK

This deep-dwelling, eel-like shark has a mouth lined with hundreds of triple-spiked teeth. The multiple rows of teeth are good for grabbing and holding slippery squid.

FRILLED SHARK

STATS

6	SPEED
5	STRENGTH
3	BRAINS
6	ATTACK
6	DEFENSE

SCIENTIFIC NAME	*Chlamydoselachus anguineus*
LENGTH	3–5 feet (91–152 cm)
TYPICAL PREY	Squid, fish, other sharks; may also eat carrion that drift down to the depths
PREDATOR STYLE	Slow swimmer, probably unable to chase fast-moving prey
WATER TYPE	Salt

WHO WINS?
SEE PAGE 111.

JAGUAR VS. BURMESE PYTHON

JAGUAR

Like most animals in the cat family, the jaguar spends almost all of its time alone. This strikingly beautiful predator has tremendous jaws that it uses to clamp onto prey. Its strong jaw muscles can easily break a turtle's shell.

SCIENTIFIC NAME	*Panthera onca*
LENGTH (WITHOUT TAIL)	5–6 feet (1.5–1.8 m)
TYPICAL PREY	Fish, turtles, caimans, deer
PREDATOR STYLE	Ambushes and pounces; kills with a powerful bite
HABITAT	Central and South America (mainly Amazon basin)

JAGUAR

STATS		
SPEED		7
STRENGTH		7
BRAINS		7
ATTACK		8
DEFENSE		7

THE SHOWDOWN

The jaguar and the python are two stealthy and solitary hunters. Both are good swimmers. Both have big jaws and a mean bite. In a head-to-head battle, which would come out on top?

BURMESE PYTHON

One of the largest snakes in the world, the Burmese python can eat an animal five times the size of its head! Its jaws unhinge so that it can swallow prey whole.

BURMESE PYTHON

STATS

5	SPEED	
6	STRENGTH	
4	BRAINS	
8	ATTACK	
6	DEFENSE	

SCIENTIFIC NAME	*Python molurus bivittatus*
LENGTH	16–23 feet (4.9–7 m)
TYPICAL PREY	Rabbits, mice, rats, lizards, snakes, birds
PREDATOR STYLE	Stalks, bites, and squeezes until prey suffocates
HABITAT	Southeast Asia

WHO WINS?
SEE PAGE 111.

GANGES RIVER DOLPHIN VS. GHARIAL

GANGES RIVER DOLPHIN

This endangered mammal is almost blind, but eyes aren't much use anyway in the muddy water where it lives. Instead, it "sees" with echolocation (sonar).

SCIENTIFIC NAME	*Platanista gangetica*
LENGTH	7–11.5 feet (2.1–3.5 m)
TYPICAL PREY	Bottom-dwelling crustaceans, mollusks, fish
PREDATOR STYLE	Hunts by echolocation (sonar) along the river bottom
WATER TYPE	Fresh

GANGES RIVER DOLPHIN

STATS

SPEED	8
STRENGTH	7
BRAINS	9
ATTACK	5
DEFENSE	5

THE SPLASHDOWN

Two long-snouted riverdwellers from South Asia meet in this Indian splashdown. The Ganges River dolphin hunts fish, mollusks, and crustaceans in the muddy river that gives it its name. The gharial's narrow, toothy snout is built for whipping quickly sideways through the water.

GHARIAL

The gharial is one of the biggest members of the crocodile family. It's fast and agile in the water but a slow mover on land.

GHARIAL

STATS

6	SPEED	
8	STRENGTH	
	4	BRAINS
6	ATTACK	
7	DEFENSE	

SCIENTIFIC NAME	*Gavialis gangeticus*
LENGTH	13–20 feet (4–6.1 m)
TYPICAL PREY	Fish
PREDATOR STYLE	Ambush hunter; waits motionless in water, then whips snout sideways to snap up passing fish
WATER TYPE	Fresh

WHO WINS?
SEE PAGE 111.

FRESH WATER

Only about 3 percent of the water on the surface of the earth is fresh water. But the animals that live and hunt there can be just as large and fearsome as saltwater predators.

Some of them also hunt in brackish water, which means water that is slightly salty. Brackish water is found in estuaries, where rivers meet the ocean.

These are some of the special weapons used by splashdown predators that live or hunt at least some of the time in freshwater streams, rivers, and lakes.

VENOMOUS SPURS

PLATYPUS

VENOMOUS STING

FRESHWATER STINGRAY

TEETH

CROCODILE

LURE ON TONGUE

ALLIGATOR SNAPPING TURTLE

VENOMOUS BITE

COTTONMOUTH

CONSTRICTING COILS

GREEN ANACONDA

BULL SHARK VS. ALLIGATOR GAR

BULL SHARK

This saltwater predator can travel long distances up freshwater rivers. Bull sharks have been found up to 2,500 miles (4,023 km) from the ocean.

SCIENTIFIC NAME	*Carcharhinus leucas*
LENGTH	7–11 feet (2.1–3.4 m)
TYPICAL PREY	Fish of all types, including stingrays and smaller sharks
PREDATOR STYLE	Hunts along the ocean and river bottoms, pursues prey with quick bursts of speed
WATER TYPE	Salt/Fresh

BULL SHARK

STATS

SPEED	8
STRENGTH	8
BRAINS	6
ATTACK	9
DEFENSE	9

THE SPLASHDOWN

The saltwater bull shark travels up the river to face off against the alligator gar. The bull shark is one of the most dangerous sharks in the world to humans. Is the alligator gar as tough as it looks?

ALLIGATOR GAR

The alligator gar is one of the biggest freshwater fish in North America. It often floats like a log near the water's surface to ambush prey.

ALLIGATOR GAR

STATS

5	SPEED	
6	STRENGTH	
4	BRAINS	
6	ATTACK	
6	DEFENSE	

SCIENTIFIC NAME	*Atractosteus spatula*
LENGTH	6–10 feet (1.8–3 m)
TYPICAL PREY	Fish, crabs, sometimes birds
PREDATOR STYLE	Ambush hunter; floats motionless in wait for prey
WATER TYPE	Fresh

WHO WINS?
SEE PAGE 111.

KOMODO DRAGON VS. TIGER

KOMODO DRAGON

Komodo dragons' bites are almost always fatal. Venom sends prey into shock, and killer bacteria in the dragon's saliva means prey animals always die of their wounds, even if they escape from an attack.

SCIENTIFIC NAME	*Varanus komodoensis*
LENGTH	10 feet (3 m), including tail
TYPICAL PREY	Deer, boar, water buffalo
PREDATOR STYLE	Stealth, deadly bite; eats almost all of prey, including hide and hooves
HABITAT	Small islands of Indonesia

KOMODO DRAGON

STATS

SPEED	4
STRENGTH	5
BRAINS	2
ATTACK	9
DEFENSE	4

THE SHOWDOWN

Two evenly matched giants that inspire fear and wonder, the world's largest lizard and the world's largest cat face off. They're both ambush hunters, but while tigers rely on their jaws, Komodo dragons count on something even more lethal.

TIGER

Tigers are the undisputed rulers of the Asian jungles they call home. After lying in wait, a charging tiger knocks its prey to the ground and then clamps its crushing jaws to the struggling animal's throat to suffocate it.

TIGER

STATS

7	SPEED	
7	STRENGTH	
	6	BRAINS
8	ATTACK	
	4	DEFENSE

SCIENTIFIC NAME	*Panthera tigris*
LENGTH	8 feet (2.4 m), including tail
TYPICAL PREY	Deer, boar, water buffalo
PREDATOR STYLE	Ambush, power; drags prey to a hidden spot before eating
HABITAT	India, Southeast Asia, and the Russian Far East

WHO WINS?
SEE PAGE 111.

COTTONMOUTH VS. ALLIGATOR SNAPPING TURTLE

COTTONMOUTH

The cottonmouth gets its name from the warning it gives when threatened: it opens its jaws to show off fangs and the white-colored lining of its mouth.

SCIENTIFIC NAME	*Agkistrodon piscivorus*
LENGTH	3–6 feet (91–183 cm)
TYPICAL PREY	Fish, amphibians, reptiles, birds, small mammals
PREDATOR STYLE	Subdues prey with venomous bite; detects warm-blooded prey with heat-sensing organs in its face
WATER TYPE	Fresh

COTTONMOUTH

STATS		
SPEED		7
STRENGTH	5	
BRAINS	4	
ATTACK		8
DEFENSE		8

THE SPLASHDOWN

It's a splashdown in the swamp as these two North American reptiles face off. The venomous cottonmouth, or water moccasin, is a relative of the rattlesnake. The alligator snapping turtle is the largest freshwater turtle in the Americas.

ALLIGATOR SNAPPING TURTLE

This huge turtle opens its mouth underwater to show a bright pink, worm-shaped lure on its tongue. Any prey that comes close to investigate gets snapped up.

ALLIGATOR SNAPPING TURTLE

STATS

5	SPEED	
7	STRENGTH	
4	BRAINS	
6	ATTACK	
6	DEFENSE	

SCIENTIFIC NAME	*Macrochelys temminckii*
LENGTH	2–2.5 feet (61–76 cm) shell length
TYPICAL PREY	Fish, frogs, snakes, crayfish, other turtles, plants
PREDATOR STYLE	Attracts prey with lure in mouth
WATER TYPE	Fresh

WHO WINS?
SEE PAGE 111.

GOLIATH TIGERFISH VS. JAPANESE GIANT SALAMANDER

GOLIATH TIGERFISH

This toothy river dweller lurks in eddies and calm areas of whitewater rapids. When it spots a fish, it chases down its prey with a burst of speed.

SCIENTIFIC NAME	*Hydrocynus goliath*
LENGTH	4–5 feet (1.2–1.5 m)
TYPICAL PREY	Fish
PREDATOR STYLE	Ambush hunter
WATER TYPE	Fresh

GOLIATH TIGERFISH

STATS

SPEED	7
STRENGTH	7
BRAINS	4
ATTACK	7
DEFENSE	7

THE SPLASHDOWN

Predators from opposite sides of the world match fighting skills in a freshwater splashdown. The goliath tigerfish lives in Africa's Congo River basin. The giant salamander, the world's second-largest amphibian, lives in the mountain streams of Japan.

JAPANESE GIANT SALAMANDER

This huge amphibian is nearly blind. It navigates and hunts in the water using its other senses, including special vibration-sensing cells in its skin.

JAPANESE GIANT SALAMANDER

STATS		
4	SPEED	
5	STRENGTH	
4	BRAINS	
4	ATTACK	
4	DEFENSE	

SCIENTIFIC NAME	*Andrias japonicus*
LENGTH	5 feet (1.5 m)
TYPICAL PREY	Fish, insects, crustaceans, anything else it can catch
PREDATOR STYLE	Hunts using senses of smell, touch, and vibration-detecting cells in skin
WATER TYPE	Fresh

WHO WINS?
SEE PAGE 111.

WHO WOULD WIN?

The experts pick their champions. Do you agree?

pp. 8–9
GRIZZLY BEAR VS. MOUNTAIN LION
The cougar is a top predator, but the grizzly simply overmatches it.

pp. 10–11
ORCA VS. GREAT WHITE SHARK
In a ferocious battle, the killer whale finally gets the upper hand. The orca wins the splashdown.

pp. 12–13
AMERICAN ALLIGATOR VS. SALTWATER CROCODILE
In this brute-force contest, size and weight make all the difference. The croc wins the splashdown by a chomp!

pp. 14–15
FAT-TAILED SCORPION VS. HORNED BABOON TARANTULA
The scorpion can strike faster than the tarantula, and its shell is strong, providing good protection against the tarantula's bite.

pp. 16–17
NILE CROCODILE VS. HIPPOPOTAMUS
Even the biggest crocodile has a hard time standing up to a full-grown hippo. The hippopotamus wins with a tank-like charge and a hippo-sized chomp.

pp. 18–19
HONEY BADGER VS. WOLVERINE
The honey badger is incredibly aggressive, but the wolverine has a bigger mouth and a stronger bite. The honey badger's smaller mouth and teeth just can't compete with the wolverine's larger weapons.

pp. 20–21
POLAR BEAR VS. WALRUS
The bear charges, but the walrus flops into the water just in time. The bear is a good swimmer, but the walrus can dive deeper and stay under longer. The contest is a tie.

pp. 24–25
BLUE-RINGED OCTOPUS VS. REEF STONEFISH
The stonefish is larger, but its spines work only for defense, not attack. The tiny octopus wins the battle with its deadly bite.

pp. 26–27
CHINESE PRAYING MANTIS VS. ASIAN GIANT HORNET
The praying mantis is a great hunter, but before it could deliver a killing bite to its opponent's head, the hornet's sting would paralyze it.

pp. 28–29
GREAT BARRACUDA VS. GRAY REEF SHARK
Size, power, and aggressiveness triumph over speed in this contest. The shark is the winner.

pp. 30–31
GOLDEN JACKAL VS. PUFF ADDER
This is a tough battle between two tough predators. Although the jackal is used to hunting and eating snakes, it can't handle the adder's deadly venom.

pp. 32–33
ELECTRIC EEL VS. RED-BELLIED PIRANHA
The electric eel zaps the whole pack of piranhas at the same time. The showdown is over in moments, with the eel victorious.

pp. 34–35
GRAY WOLF VS. AFRICAN LEOPARD
The leopard has a bigger bite and larger canine teeth. Unlike the wolf, it can fight with its powerful forepaws.

pp. 36–37
GOLDEN EAGLE VS. GREAT HORNED OWL
These two raptors are well matched. However, the eagle has the edge because it is bigger and can maneuver better in the air.

pp. 40–41
GREEN ANACONDA VS. ARAPAIMA
The lurking anaconda grabs the arapaima when it surfaces to breathe. The fish succumbs to the unyielding grip of the snake's squeezing coils.

pp. 42–43
FISHER VS. RED FOX
The fisher puts up a good fight, but it can't get past the fox's bigger bite.

pp. 44–45
SPERM WHALE VS. GIANT SQUID
The squid puts up a ferocious fight, but the whale's peg-toothed jaw stays clamped on the mollusk's body. The whale gets a squid dinner.

pp. 46–47
STOAT VS. YELLOW MONGOOSE
This would be a tough fight for both animals, but in the end, the mongoose is the more aggressive fighter and would win the match.

pp. 48–49
GIANT MORAY VS. LONGFIN EEL
In spite of the giant moray's fiercer looks, these two are about as evenly matched as a pair of eels from different habitats can be. The contest ends in a tie.

pp. 50–51
GREAT HAMMERHEAD VS. LEMON SHARK
The lemon shark puts up a good fight, but in the end, it is no match for the larger, agile hammerhead. The great hammerhead is victorious.

pp. 54–55
TASMANIAN DEVIL VS. DINGO
The Tasmanian devil has a tremendous bite, but the dingo has size and large canine teeth on its side. The devil is tenacious, and the dingo would suffer a lot of damage. In the end, these two, this time, part ways with neither one claiming victory.

pp. 56–57
BLUE MARLIN VS. SWORDFISH
Superior size and strength carry the day. The victory goes to the blue marlin.

pp. 58–59
PLATYPUS VS. NEEDLEFISH
The needlefish snaps with its jaws but doesn't use its beak as an offensive stabbing weapon. The platypus's venomous spurs give it the edge in the fight. The platypus wins.

pp. 60–61
RETICULATED PYTHON VS. KING COBRA
The python is a constrictor, and it usually hunts mammals. It would be harder for it to constrict a snake. The cobra, however, specializes in killing other snakes. With its quick strike, long fangs, and extremely strong venom, it would be the winner in this face-off.

pp. 62–63
PEREGRINE FALCON VS. BOBCAT
The falcon is strong and fast, and it might be able to injure the bobcat, but the bobcat has greater size, powerful paws, and sharp teeth.

pp. 64–65
BLUEFIN TUNA VS. LIONFISH
The lionfish keeps to the crevices of its coral-reef habitat, where the huge tuna can't follow. The lionfish's venomous sting sends the tuna on a hasty retreat.

pp. 66–67
BULLET ANT VS. ASSASSIN BUG
The ant's venomous sting gives it the edge in this fight.

pp. 70–71
NORTHERN STARGAZER VS. PACIFIC ELECTRIC RAY
Even though both opponents can produce a 50-volt zap, the electric ray packs more power into its jolts. The victory goes to the ray.

pp. 72–73
LION VS. SPOTTED HYENA
The lion is known as the king of the beasts for a reason. Even against the hyena's superior speed and strength, the lion's powerful attack means triumph for the cat.

pp. 74–75
BANDED SEA KRAIT VS. SEA SNAKE
The sea krait's larger size gives it the advantage, but the yellow-bellied sea snake can stay below the surface longer. The splashdown ends in a draw.

pp. 76–77
RABID WOLF SPIDER VS. BLACK WIDOW
The black widow's venom is no match for the wolf spider's bite.

pp. 78–79
GIANT PACIFIC OCTOPUS VS. HARBOR SEAL
In an underwater wrestling match, the seal barely escapes from the octopus's powerful grip in time to reach the surface to breathe. The octopus is the winner.

pp. 80–81
OSPREY VS. BALD EAGLE
These animals are very evenly matched. However, eagles are known to pester osprey and steal fish from them. With its size and weight advantage, the bald eagle takes the win.

pp. 82–83
BALLOONFISH VS. OYSTER TOADFISH
With its opponent puffed out like a prickly balloon, the toadfish can't get past the spines for a bite. The contest goes to the balloonfish.

pp. 86–87
GIANT OTTER VS. STINGRAY
The otter dives in for a direct attack, only to get a jab from the stingray's venomous barb. The otter retreats in pain, and the ray wins the day.

pp. 88–89
SERVAL VS. CHEETAH
The relatively small-boned cat is bigger and more powerful. Not even the serval's amazing leaps can save it.

pp. 90–91
ANGLERFISH VS. PELICAN EEL
Glowing lures work best when the prey is smaller than the predator. The gulper eel zeroes in on the anglerfish's lure and swallows its opponent with a single gulp.

pp. 92–93
PORTUGUESE MAN-OF-WAR VS. BOX JELLYFISH
The box jellyfish can swim, while the man-of-war can only drift with the wind and currents. The more maneuverable box jellyfish is victorious.

pp. 94–95
PACIFIC BLACKDRAGON VS. FRILLED SHARK
The blackdragon has the speed, but it doesn't have a big enough mouth to cause much harm to the shark. The battle ends in a draw.

pp. 96–97
JAGUAR VS. BURMESE PYTHON
Jaguars are good at hunting snakes, pythons in particular. The cat's powerful jaws could easily crush the snake's skull.

pp. 98–99
GANGES RIVER DOLPHIN VS. GHARIAL
The gharial's motionless ambush method doesn't fool the dolphin's sonar sense. Victory goes to the dolphin.

pp. 102–103
BULL SHARK VS. ALLIGATOR GAR
The alligator gar can't get the better of the faster, heavier bull shark. The shark wins the splashdown.

pp. 104–105
KOMODO DRAGON VS. TIGER
The tiger is much stronger and more agile than the dragon, but one bite from the dragon could spell doom for the tiger. The tiger kills the dragon, but it dies days later from an infected bite.

pp. 106–107
COTTONMOUTH VS. ALLIGATOR SNAPPING TURTLE
The turtle pulls into its shell to protect itself. When the snake's strike misses, the turtle wins the contest with one snapping chomp.

pp. 108–109
GOLIATH TIGERFISH VS. JAPANESE GIANT SALAMANDER
The nearly sightless salamander can't keep up with the sharp-eyed tigerfish. The victory goes to the tigerfish.

Brimming with creative inspiration, how-to projects, and useful information to enrich your everyday life, Quarto Knows is a favorite destination for those pursuing their interests and passions. Visit our site and dig deeper with our books into your area of interest: Quarto Creates, Quarto Cooks, Quarto Homes, Quarto Lives, Quarto Drives, Quarto Explores, Quarto Gifts, or Quarto Kids.

First Published in 2017 by becker&mayer! books, an imprint of The Quarto Group.
11120 NE 33rd Place, Suite 101
Bellevue, WA 98004
www.QuartoKnows.com

becker&mayer! kids titles are also available at discount for retail, wholesale, promotional, and bulk purchase. For details, contact the Special Sales Manager by email at specialsales@quarto.com or by mail at The Quarto Group, Attn: Special Sales Manager, 401 Second Avenue North, Suite 310, Minneapolis, MN 55401 USA.

17 18 19 20 21   5 4 3 2 1

ISBN: 978-0-7603-5535-0

Library of Congress Cataloging-in-Publication Data is available.

Authors: Paul Beck and Lee Martin
Editorial: Ashley McPhee
Production: Cindy Curren

Printed, manufactured, and assembled in China/Shenzhen, 07/17.

MIX
Paper from responsible sources
FSC® C017606

COVER: Tiger ©dptro/ Shutterstock.com, Wolf ©Eduardo Grund/ AlamyStock Photo, leopard growling ©Villiers Steyn/ Shutterstock.com.

Title Page: Alligator ©Sergei Aleshin/ Shutterstock.com, Wolf ©Eduardo Grund / Alamy Stock Photo, Tiger ©dptro/Shutterstock.co; TOC page: Shark jumping out of water ©Alexyz3d/ Shutterstock.co; Page 6: Gray wolf ©Geoffrey Kuchera/Shutterstock.co; Page 7: Grizzly bear ©Scott E Read/ Shutterstock.com, Lion ©e2dan/ Shutterstock.com, Shark ©Martin Prochazkacz/ Shutterstock.com, Killer whale ©Jan Daly/ Shutterstock.com; Page 8: Grizzly bear ©Jack Nevitt/ Shutterstock.com; Page 9: Mountain Lion ©Melanie DeFazio/ Shutterstock.com; Page 10: Orca ©Juniors Bildarchiv GmbH/ AlamyStock Photo; Page 11: Great white shark ©Ramon Carretero/ Shutterstock.com; Page 12: American Alligator ©imageBROKER /Superstock; Page 13: Saltwater Crocodile ©imageBROKER/ AlamyStock Photo; Page 14: Fat-tailed scorpion ©Dennis W Donohue/ Shutterstock.com; Page 15: Horned baboon terantula ©EcoPrint/ Shutterstock.com; Page 16: Nile Crocodile ©Todd Gustafson/Panora/ AGE Fotostock; Page 17: Hippo ©Steve Allen/ Getty Images; Page 18: Honey Badger ©Erwin Niemand/ Shutterstock.com; Page 19: Wolverine ©Michal Ninger/ Shutterstock.com; Page 20: Polar Bear ©Richard Wear/ AGE Fotostock; Page 21: Walrus ©Art Directors & TRIP / Alamy Stock Photo; Page 22: Fat tailed scorpion ©Dennis W Donohue/ Shutterstock.com, Dingo ©Tier Und Naturfotografie J und C Sohns/ Getty Images; Page 23: Honey Badger ©Erwin Niemand/ Shutterstock.com, Red Fox ©Ghost Bear/ Shutterstock.com, Bobcat ©Dennis W Donohue/ Shutterstock.com, Black Widow Spider ©Danie Spreeth Photography/ Shutterstock.com; Page 24: Blue ringed octopus ©YUSRAN ABDUL RAHMAN/ Shutterstock.com; Page 25: Reef Stonefish ©Rich Carey/ Shutterstock.com; Page 26: Chinese Praying Mantis ©Ezume Images/ Shutterstock.com; Page 27: Asian Giant Hornet ©Contrail/ Shutterstock.com; Page 28: Great Barracuda ©aquapix/ Shutterstock.com; Page 29: Gray Reef Shark ©Morenovel/ Shutterstock.com; Page 30: Golden Jackal ©belizar/ Shutterstock.com, Puff Adder ©EcoPrint/ Shutterstock.com; Page 31: Puff Adder ©blick-winkel/ AlamyStock Photo; Page 32: Electric Eel ©Amazon-Images/ AlamyStock Photo; Page 33: Red Bellied Piranha ©imageBROKER/ AlamyStock Photo; Page 34: Gray Wolf ©Bill Frische/ Shutterstock.com; Page 35: African Leopard ©Villiers Steyn/ Shutterstock.com; Page 36: Golden Eagle ©davemhuntphotography/ Shutterstock.com; Page 37: Great Horned Owl ©Joseph/ Shutterstock.com; Page 38: Anglerfish ©Dante Fenolio/ Getty Images, Frilled Shark © Gwen Lowe / SeaPics.com; Page 39: Aglerfish ©Minden Pictures/ Superstock, Pacific Blackdragon ©NORBERT WU/ MINDEN PICTURES/National Geographic Creative, Pacific Blackdragon ©Dante Fenolio/Science Source, Giant Octopus ©Dustie/ Shutterstock.com; Page 40: Green anaaconda ©JASON EDWARDS/National Geographic Creative; Page 41: Arapaima ©JAKKAPAN PRAMMANASIK/ Shutterstock.com; Page 42: Fisher ©Gaertner/ AlamyStock Photo; Page 43: Red Fox ©L Galbraith/ Shutterstock.com; Page 44: Sperm Whale ©wildestanimal/ Shutterstock.com; Page 45: Giant Squid ©Amanda Cotton/ AlamyStock Photo; Page 46: Stoat ©Bildagentur Zoonar GmbH/ Shutterstock.com; Page 47: Yellow Mongoose ©EcoPrint/ Shutterstock.com; Page 48: Moray Eel ©Rich Carey/ Shutterstock.com; Page 49: Longfin Eel ©Rafael Ben-Ari/ AlamyStock Photo; Page 50: Hammerhead Shark ©Tomas Kotouc/ Shutterstock.com; Page 51: Lemon Shark ©Michael Bogner/ Shutterstock.com; Page 52: Cheetah ©Villiers Steyn/ Shutterstock.com, Peregrine Falcon ©Brian E Kushner/ Shutterstock.com; Page 53: Chinese Praying Mantis ©Ezume Images/ Shutterstock.com, Lion ©andamanec/ Shutterstock.com, Puff Adder ©EcoPrint/ Shutterstock.com, Mongoose ©Petr Kalousek/ Shutterstock.com; Page 54: Tasmanian Devil ©Andrii Slonchak/ Shutterstock.com; Page 55: Dingo ©Tier Und Naturfotografie J und C Sohns/ Getty Images; Page 56: Blue Marlin ©WaterFrame/ AlamyStock Photo; Page 57: Swordfish: ©WaterFrame/ AlamyStock Photo"; Page 58: Platypus ©Dave Watts/ AlamyStock Photo; Page 59: Reef Needlefish ©Andrey Nekrasov/ AlamyStock Photo; Page 60: Reticulated Python ©MaxShutter/ Shutterstock.com; Page 61: King Cobra ©Clement Carbillet/ Shutterstock.com; Page 62: Peregrine Falcon ©dirkr/ Shutterstock.com; Page 63: Bobcat ©Don Mammoser/ Shutterstock.com; Page 64: Bluefin Tuna ©MISCELLANEOUSTOCK/ AlamyStock Photo; Page 65: Red Lionfish ©Dan Exton/ Shutterstock.com; Page 66: Bullet Ant ©worldswildlifewonders/ Shutterstock.com; Page 67: Assassin Bug ©kurt_G/ Shutterstock.com; Page 68: Lionfish ©Shutterstock.com, Banded Sea Krait ©Howard Chew/ Dreamstime.com, Electric Ray ©Maxim Khytra/ Shutterstock.com; Page 69: Great white shark ©Willyam Bradberry/ Shutterstock.com, jellyfish: "©Visuals Unlimited: Inc./David Fleetham/ Getty Images", polar bear ©Mirage3/ Dreamstime.com; Page 70: Northern Stargazer © Marilyn & Maris Kazmers/ SeaPics.com; Page 71: Pacific Electric Ray ©Jeff Rotman/ AlamyStock Photo; Page 72: Lion ©Neil Bradfield/ Shutterstock.com; Page 73: Hyena ©Daniel-Alvarez/ Shutterstock.com; Page 74: Banded Sea Krait ©Ethan Daniels/ Shutterstock.com; Page 75: Yellow Bellied Sea Snake ©William Mullins/ AlamyStock Photo; Page 76: Rabid Wolf Spider ©Nathanael Siders/ Shutterstock.com; Page 77: Black Widow Spider ©Sari Oneal/ Shutterstock.com; Page 78: Giant Pacific Octopus ©Mikhail Blajenov/ Dreamstime.com; Page 79: Harbor Seal ©David Osborn/ Shutterstock.com; Page 80: Osprey ©Jeff Grabert/ Shutterstock.com; Page 81: Bald Eagle ©Richard Lowthian/ Shutterstock.com; Page 82: Balloonfish ©Beth Swanson/ Shutterstock.com; Page 83: Oyster Toadfish ©Joe Quinn/ Shutterstock.com; Page 84: Reticulated Python ©RAYphotographer/ Shutterstock.com, Gray Wolf ©Jim Cumming/ Shutterstock.com; Page 85: Mountain Lion ©Shutterstock.com, Grizzly Bear ©TheWonderWays/ Shutterstock.com, Asian Giant Hornet ©J-R/ Shutterstock.com, Rabid Wolf Spider ©

©Rob Gordon/ AlamyStock Photo"; Page 86: Giant Otter ©Vladimir Wrangel/ Shutterstock.com; Page 87: Smooth backed Freshwater Stingray: "©Joel Sartore: National Geographic Photo Ark/ Getty Images"; Page 88: Serval ©Stayer/ Shutterstock.com; Page 89: Cheetah ©Lucasdm/ Shutterstock.com; Page 90: Humpback Anglerfish ©Helmut Corneli/imageb / imageBROKER ; Page 91: Pelican Eel ©Norbert Wu/ Minden Pictures/ Getty Images; Page 92: Portuguese Man-o-war ©Stephen Frink/ Getty Images; Page 94: Pacific Dragonfish ©Mark Conlin/ Getty Images; Page 95: Frilled Shark ©Getty Images / Staff; Page 96: Jaguar ©Joe Austin Photography/ AlamyStock Photo; Page 97: Burmese Python ©LesPalenik/ Shutterstock.com; Page 98: Ganges River dolphin ©Roland Seitre/ Minden Pictures/ Getty Images; Page 99: Gharial ©LesPalenik/ Shutterstock.com; Page 100: Platypus ©worldswildlifewonders/ Shutterstock.com, Freshwater Stingray ©NHPA / NHPA/ SuperStock; Page 101: Crocoile ©prochasson frederic/ Shutterstock.com, Alligator Snapping Turtle ©Ryan M. Bolton/ Shutterstock.com, Cottonmouth ©Spllogics/ Dreamstime.com, Green anaconda ©reptiles4all/ Shutterstock.com; Page 102: Bull shark ©Bluehand/ Dreamstime.com; Page 103: Alligator Gar ©Michael Durham/ Minden Pictures/ Getty Images; Page 104: Komodo Dragon ©Patrick Rolands/ Shutterstock.com; Page 105: Tiger ©cesurkuchuk/ Shutterstock.com; Page 106: Cottonmouth ©Gerald A. DeBoer/ Shutterstock.com; Page 107: Alligator Snapping Turtle ©Lukas Blazek/ Dreamstime.com; Page 108: Goliath Tiger Fish ©Gerard Lacz Images/SuperStock; Page 109: Japanese Giant Salamander ©Cyril Ruoso/ Minden Pictures/ Getty Images.

Back Cover: Great white shark ©Ramon Carretero/ Shutterstock.com.

All design elements provided by: ©Shutterstock.com

171032